Mountains

by Rachel Sparks Linfield

Contents

Section 1
Introducing Mountains	2
Living on Mountains	7

Section 2
Climbing Mountains	12
Mountain Sports	17

Section 3
Surviving Mountain Weather	21
Mountain Rescues	27

Glossary	31
Index	32

Longman

Edinburgh Gate
Harlow, Essex

Introducing Mountains

What is a mountain?

A mountain is a hill that is more than 600 metres higher than the land around it. If it is less than 600 metres high it is just called a hill.

Where can mountains be found?

About one twentieth of the Earth's land surface is made up of mountains. Mountains can be found all over the world. Some mountains are part of **mountain ranges**. The largest mountain ranges are:

❖ the Rockies in North America

❖ the Andes in South America

❖ the Alps in Europe

❖ the Himalayas in Asia.

Which is the highest mountain in the world?

Mount Everest is said to be the highest mountain. It is part of the Himalayas and is 8849 metres above sea level. Mauna Kea in Hawaii is 10 000 metres high, but about 6000 metres of this mountain are below the sea.

Mount Everest

Even taller mountains can be found on other planets in the solar system. The largest mountain on Mars is Olympus Mons. It measures 27 000 metres above the surface of Mars. This is over three times the height of Mount Everest!

Olympus Mons

How long does it take for a mountain to form?

It takes millions of years for a mountain to form. Scientists study the types of rocks that mountains are made from to work out their ages. This table shows the ages of some mountain ranges.

Mountain range	Age in millions of years
Highlands (in Scotland)	400
Andes (in South America)	80
Himalayas (in Asia)	40
Alps (in Europe)	15

Were all mountains formed in the same way?

The Earth's surface is made up of about 15 pieces called plates. Almost all mountains formed at the edges of these plates. Mountains have been made in a number of ways. These include fold mountains, block mountains and volcanic mountains.

Fold mountains

Fold mountains were made when pieces of the Earth's surface pushed together. This is how mountain ranges like the Alps and the Andes were formed.

You can use plasticine and two blocks of wood to see how a fold mountain was formed:

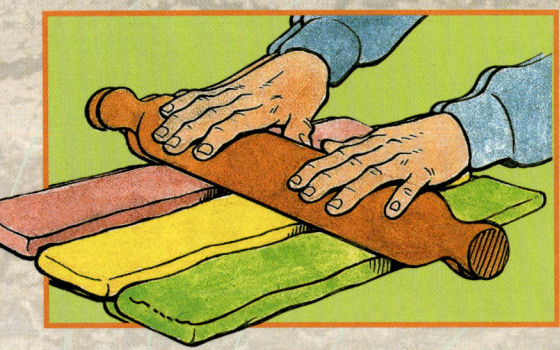

1 Roll out three thick layers of plasticine.

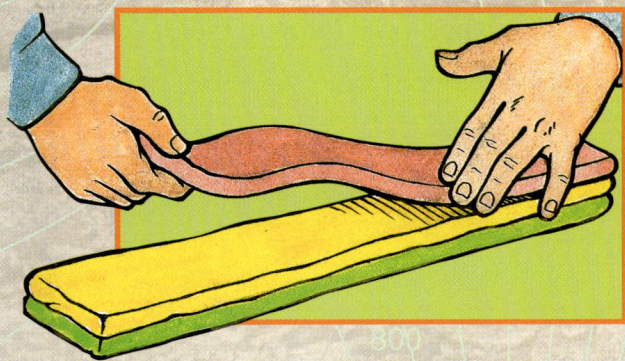

2 Place the layers on top of each other.

3 Lay the plasticine between the two blocks.

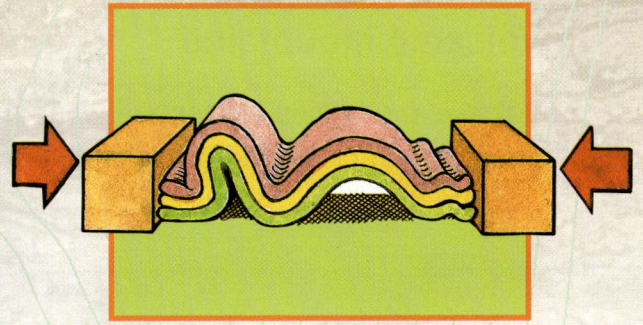

4 Push the blocks. The harder you push, the more the plasticine will fold.

About 50 million years ago the map of our world would have looked different. India was an island at this time. The Himalayas were made when India crashed into Asia and the rock was pushed upwards.

Mount Everest is a fold mountain that is still growing. Each year it grows by about one centimetre!

Block mountains

When pressure builds up inside the Earth, rocks can crack. If the cracks are too close together the piece of **crust** between them may slip down or be pushed up. If a large chunk is pushed up it forms a block mountain.

A block mountain

Volcanic mountains

Volcanic mountains are formed when **molten** rock escapes through a crack in the Earth's crust and gathers on the surface.

A volcanic mountain

Living on Mountains

As you go up a mountain it becomes colder and there is less **oxygen**. This can make it difficult for animals to live and for plants to grow. Mountain plants and animals have to be able to cope with low temperatures and less oxygen.

There is little life where there is always snow and ice.

The tree line: trees will not grow above this height.

In the spring snow melts and waters the meadows.

Lichens take water and goodness from moisture in the air. They grow well in mountain areas because the air is so clean.

Spring flowers attract insects.

Which animals live in the mountains?

Mountain animals that live at great heights need large hearts and lungs. Large hearts can carry more blood. This means that more oxygen is carried around the bodies. The animals also need to be able to cope with steep slopes.

Mountain goats

Mountain goats usually live in the area above the tree line. Here they can find lichens and mosses to eat. Goats have thick, fur coats to keep them warm. Rubbery pads on their hooves help the goats to grip and jump. They can jump more than three metres.

Rock crawlers

Rock crawlers are insects. They die if the temperature rises above 10 degrees centigrade. They are related to crickets and live in icy, snowy areas.

Snow leopards

Snow leopards survive well in snowy areas. This is because the angle of their legs lets them leap up to heights of 15 metres. This is very useful for hunting.

Ptarmigan

When winter comes some birds have to fly from the mountains to warmer places. The ptarmigan does not. Its toes are covered with stiff feathers that help keep the bird warm. In winter it turns from a grey brown colour to white. This means it is not easy for other animals to see the ptarmigan in the snow.

Which plants grow well on mountains?

Because mountains can be very cold and windy, mountain plants do best if they grow in low clumps. Fine hairs on their leaves help the plants to trap warmth and moisture. The hairs can also protect the plants from strong sunlight and nibbling animals.

hairs

Edelweiss　　　　　　　　　　**Gentian**

Some plants have dark colours. Dark colours absorb more heat than lighter ones. You can check this yourself. On a sunny day put a dark and a light coloured piece of paper outside. Leave them for about one hour. You will find that the dark paper feels warmer than the light one. In the same way dark coloured mountain flowers are good at absorbing heat.

What is lichen?

Lichen looks like a plant but is actually made up of a **fungus** and an **alga**. You can only see the separate fungus and alga under a microscope. Together, the alga and the fungus help each other to survive.

Lichen can grow on stone because it is very good at absorbing sunlight, which gives it energy. It will only grow in places where the air is clean. This is why lichen grows well in mountain areas.

Climbing Mountains

Many people enjoy climbing mountains for fun and for a challenge. Mountains are all different so different skills may be needed to climb each one. Mountain climbers need to be supple and have a good sense of balance. They also need to be sensible, plan their climbs and be well-equipped.

Some people like to climb on their own. They enjoy the sense of being alone and the silence at the top of a mountain. Others work well climbing with friends, trusting each other to give support over the tricky areas.

Climbers on Mount Snowdon in Wales

How do people climb icy mountains?

Ice is very slippery and difficult to walk on because there is little **friction**. Therefore, in order to climb icy mountains, climbers need help to get a good grip.

The jagged edge of the ice axe is used for gripping.

The spade-shaped edge is used for chopping ice.

Rigid climbing boots provide support for ankles.

Crampons attached to the boots can be kicked against the ice to get a grip.

For their safety, mountain climbers need other equipment:

❖ a rucksack to carry emergency supplies and climbing equipment

❖ a helmet to protect the head

❖ a climbing harness

❖ karabiners – these are used to connect climbing equipment such as ropes and the harness around a mountaineer's waist; the strongest karabiners can support up to 2250 kilograms

❖ a warm, waterproof jacket.

How are ropes used to climb mountains?

Ropes can provide security for mountaineers. Climbers are often roped together so that if one slips others can pull on the rope and break the fall.

The method used when two climbers are roped together is known as "belaying". The first climber attaches a rope to a piece of metal or sticking-out rock. The rope is then threaded through a safety catch attached to the first climber's harness and then through the second climber's harness. The first climber guides the rope whilst the second climber climbs.

How do mountaineers grip when crampons and ice axes cannot be used?

There are times when mountaineers can only grip by forcing their hands or even just their fingers into a tiny crack. This can be very painful and cause cuts and scars. But it can also keep a climber alive and stop a deadly fall!

Famous mountaineers

Over the years many people have had the urge to be the first person to climb a particular mountain, and also to climb it in a certain way. Each time a record is broken someone is likely to try and better it.

Many dangerous mountains throughout the world have now been climbed. Mountaineers have even managed to reach **summits** where breathing is difficult, without carrying additional oxygen.

22 May 1970

Vertical triumph!

On 21 May Dougal Haston and Don Whillans stood on the summit of Annapurna in the Himalayas. They were unroped and had not used additional oxygen to reach the top. They climbed the south-facing, almost vertical, 3600 metres wall of rock and ice. They climbed through dreadful weather and fierce winds.

Mountain Sports

Many years ago people had to find ways to travel across mountains in order to trade goods. People tried different ways to travel quickly and to use the heights of mountains and the snow to their advantage. These different methods have developed into sports such as skiing, abseiling, canyoning, tobogganing, mountain biking and modern rock climbing. Each year many people take holidays to enjoy challenging mountain sports.

Skiing

People have used skis to travel down mountains for over 4000 years. At first skis were just used for travelling as quickly as possible over snowy ground. In the 1840s people started to ski in competitions. Today skiing is a very popular part of the Winter Olympics.

Cross-country skiing involves travelling across gently sloping or flat ground. Cross-country skis are usually long, narrow and light. To help the skier push forward only the toe of the shoe is fixed to the ski.

Snowboarding

Many people say that it is easier and quicker to learn to snowboard than to ski.

Snowboarding probably began in the 1960s when Sherman Poppen, an American man, watched his daughter Wendy trying to stand on her sledge as she slid down a hill. Poppen took a pair of children's skis and screwed them together with a piece of doweling. Other people liked what they saw and wanted to have a go. Wendy's joined-together skis became known as a "snurfer", a word formed by combining surfer and snow.

Since then more sophisticated snowboards have been developed and in 1998 snowboarding became a Winter Olympic event for the first time.

Abseiling

Abseiling involves using a rope and braking system to travel slowly down a steep part of a mountain. Mountaineers will often use abseiling to descend parts of mountains they have climbed.

Abseiling is also a separate sport where people climb to great heights simply to abseil down. Although it can be easy to learn how to abseil, abseiling down mountains can be very dangerous and people have to think carefully about safety.

Mountain biking

Mountain bikes were first made in California in the 1970s. For the bikes to be able to travel over mountain ground they have to:

❖ be light enough to carry

❖ have rugged tyres for travelling over rocky ground

❖ have strong frames for going over rough ground and at steep angles

❖ have many gears for going up and down steep terrain

❖ have efficient brakes.

Some bike frames weigh only 1.2 kilograms. This is just a little heavier than one bag of sugar!

Sport and tourism

Whether they are looking for sport, fantastic views or new experiences, mountains have much to offer to tourists. During the winter months there are snow sports and snow-filled scenery. During the summer there is walking, climbing and sightseeing. In the mountains tourists can be as active or as lazy as they like!

Surviving Mountain Weather

Mountain conditions can be very harsh. The **summit** of Mount Everest, for example, is often at a temperature of -70 degrees centigrade. This is 70 degrees colder than the **freezing point** for water!

Mountain weather can also be extremely unpredictable. Many mountaineers begin climbs in sunny, warm weather, but are surprised to find very different weather as they climb upwards.

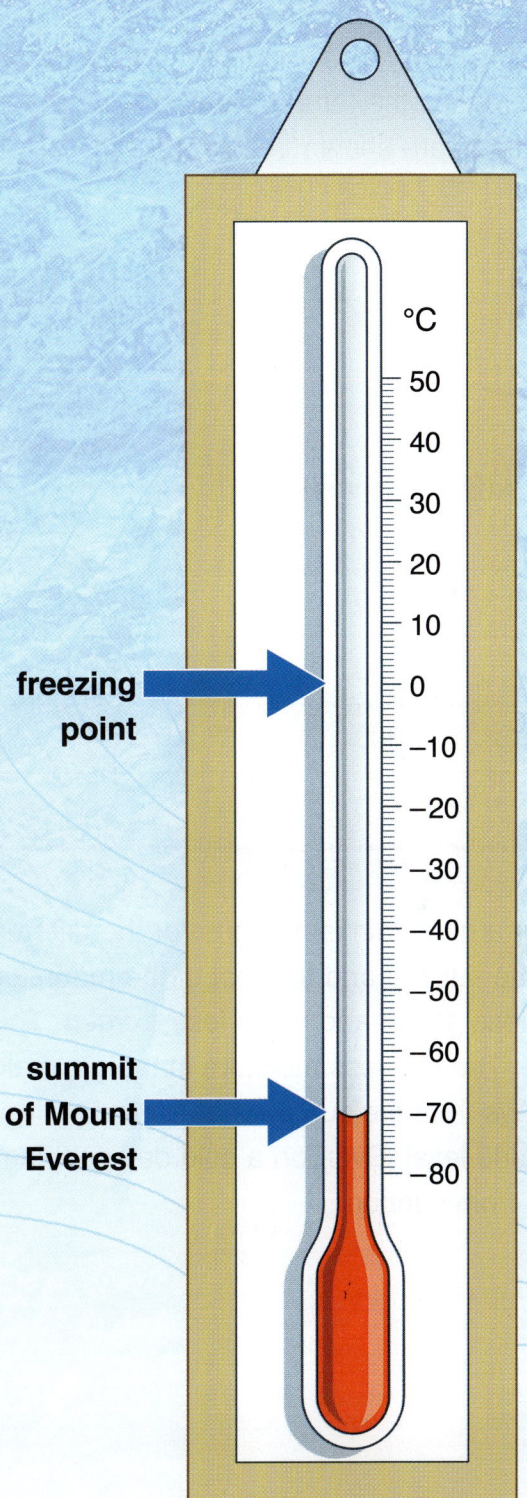

How does altitude affect mountain weather?

Altitude is the height of a mountain above sea level. As the altitude increases the temperature falls. Some typical measurements are shown in this table.

Altitude in metres	Temperature in degrees centigrade
8000	-37
5000	-17
2000	2
0	15

The higher a mountain is, the greater the difference in weather between the summit and the foot of the mountain. The air becomes less dense and holds less oxygen. This makes it difficult to breathe. There is less moisture in the air, making it feel very dry, and rays from the sun are not filtered out as much as they are at ground level. Even on a cold day people may need protection from sunburn.

Why are mountains cold?

There are a number of reasons why mountains can be cold. Two reasons are:

❖ White objects are good reflectors of heat and light. That is why white is a good colour to wear on a hot day. In the same way white snow reflects sunlight back into the atmosphere rather than absorbing it.

❖ Some northern faces of mountains are always in a shadow.

north face

Where does mountain rain fall?

Rain tends to fall only on one side of a mountain, because clouds normally blow in one direction. The drier side is called the mountain's rain shadow. The Himalayas, Andes and Rockies create very large rain shadows.

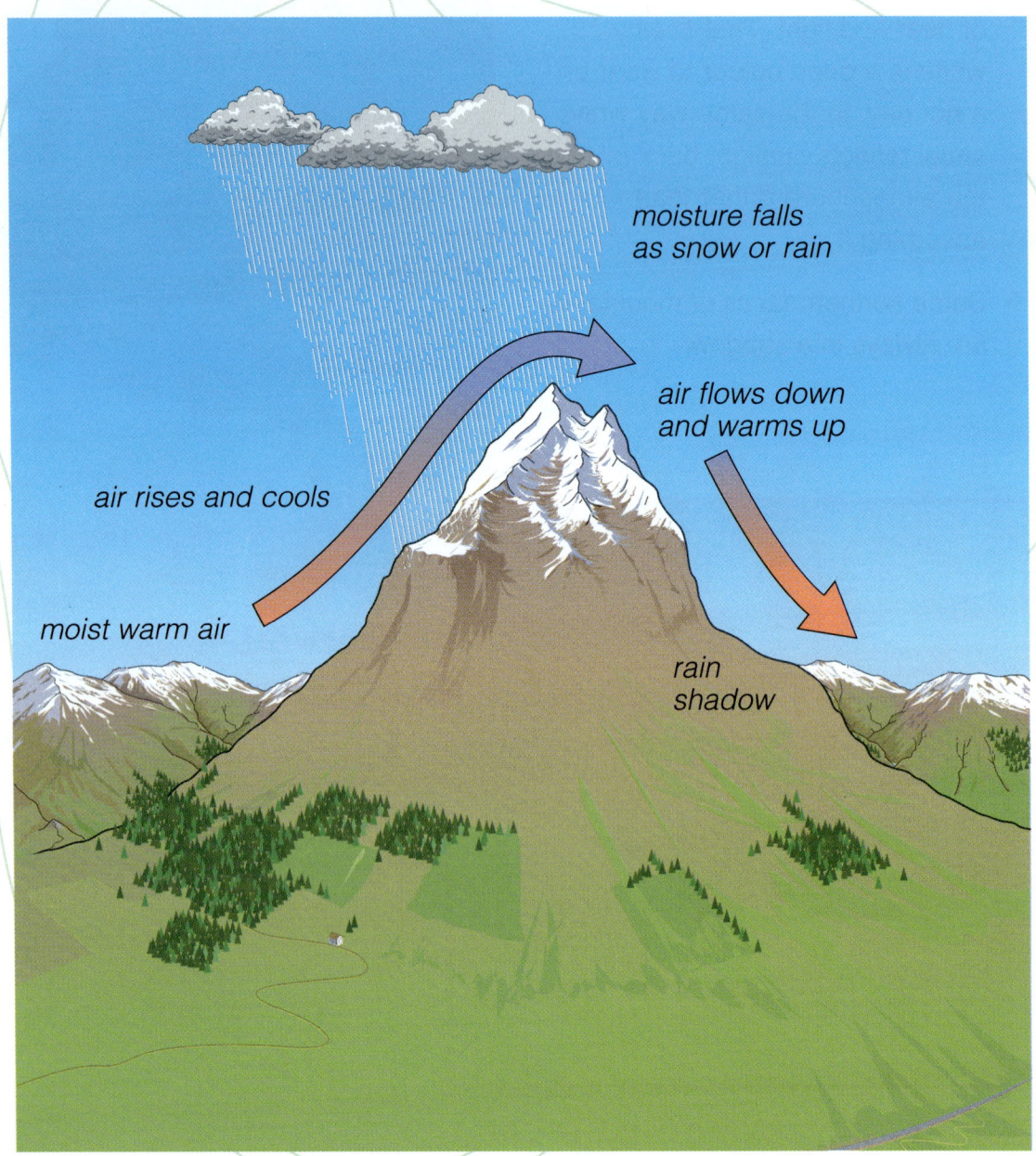

Where do avalanches happen?

Avalanches are huge masses of snow falling down the sides of mountains. They can occur in snowy, mountainous areas. The chance of one happening depends upon the:

- snow conditions
- temperature
- wind direction
- types and number of trees and plants growing
- angle of the slope.

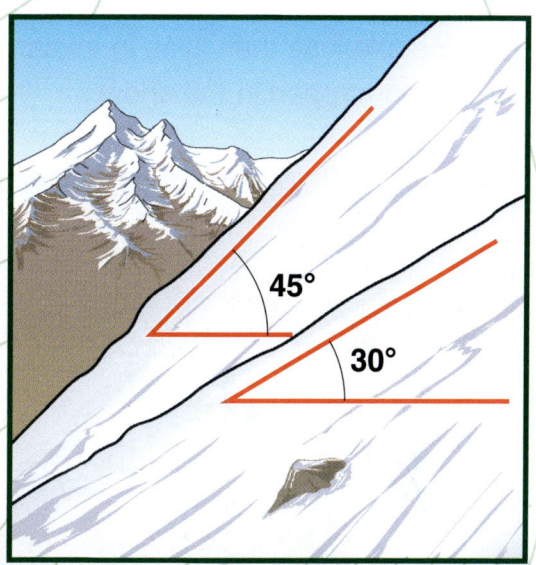

Avalanches occur most frequently on slopes that are at angles of 30° to 45° after heavy snowfalls or sudden warm weather.

As the thick blanket of snow begins to slide it pushes a huge mass of air in front of it. This creates a wind that is strong enough to flatten trees.

How can people survive an avalanche?

Skiers often say that the best way to survive an avalanche is to avoid being in it in the first place! The advice given to people going into the mountains is to learn to recognise the signs of an avalanche. They are, however, very difficult to predict. Sadly, many people lose their lives in avalanches when they become buried and trapped in the snow.

Mountain Rescues

Mountain rescue teams rescue many mountaineers each year. Some of the people rescued will have been ill-prepared for a mountain climb. Others suffer from bad weather or a freak accident. At these times mountain rescue teams may mean the difference between life and death.

Who carries out mountain rescues?

People who carry out mountain rescues are part of a team. Many of the people are volunteers who like to spend time in the mountains. The mountain rescuers have to:

- be extremely fit
- train regularly in their teams
- be very knowledgeable about the mountain areas they work in
- be qualified to give first aid.

When a rescue team is called out the team leader is responsible for organising the team members. A controller back at the rescue base maintains radio contact throughout the rescue.

The controller is also responsible for finding out as much as possible about conditions on the mountain and the person or people that need to be rescued. The controller will ensure that the rescue team are aware of any information about a person with a medical allergy (e.g. allergic to penicillin) or a particular need for medication (e.g. the person is diabetic). If necessary, controllers can organise helicopters to collect and transport casualties quickly to a hospital.

Mountain rescue equipment ready for emergency use

What equipment is necessary for a mountain rescue?

A large amount of equipment is required for rescues. This includes climbing equipment as well as things for mountain survival and first aid. The first aid equipment needed includes:

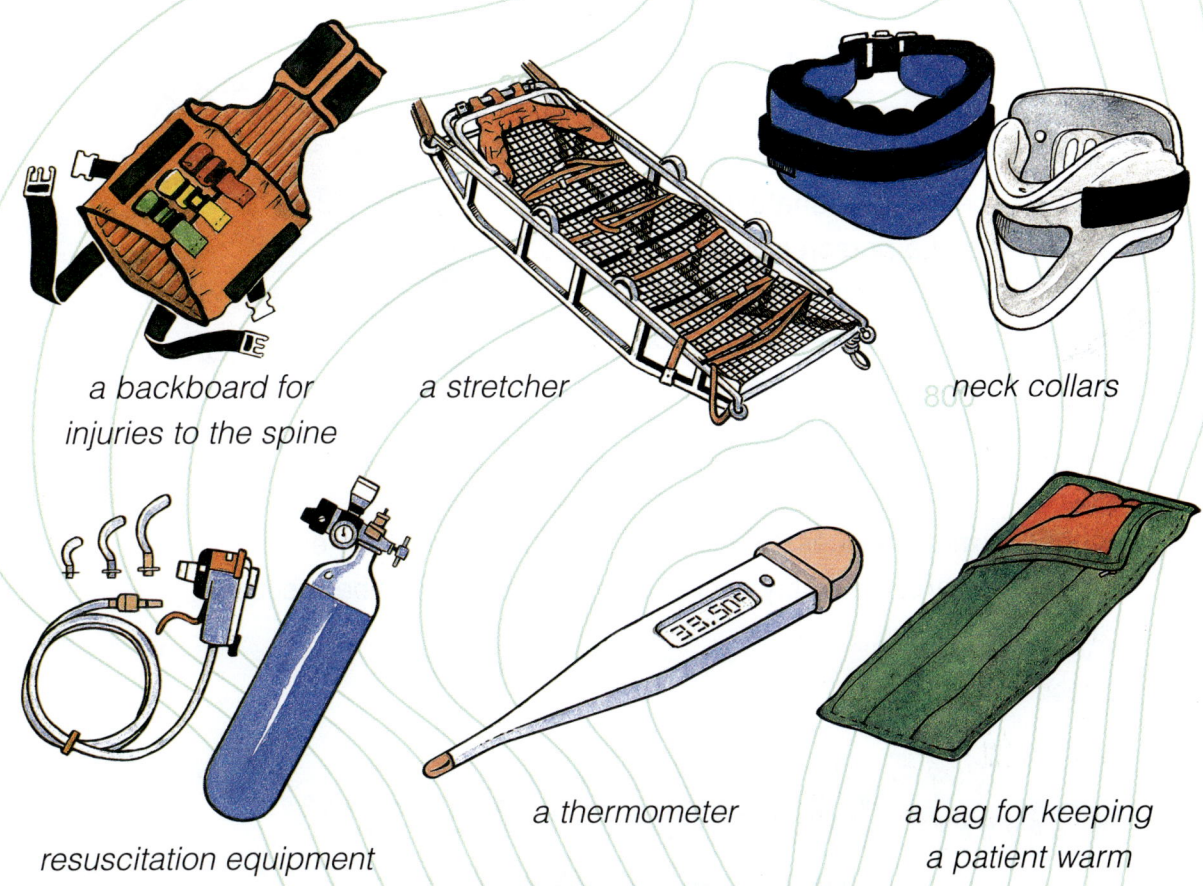

a backboard for injuries to the spine

a stretcher

neck collars

resuscitation equipment

a thermometer

a bag for keeping a patient warm

Rescuers need to be able to carry equipment weighing about 18 kilograms, which is as heavy as 18 bags of sugar!

Sometimes people waiting to be rescued suffer from hypothermia. This happens if their body temperature drops below 35 degrees centigrade. It can be caused by exhaustion or being out in very cold, wet conditions. Although people can recover from hypothermia, the quicker they are rescued and given first aid, the greater their chance of survival.

When are dogs used?

A dog's sense of smell is very much greater than that of a human being. Dogs can use their sense of smell to detect people who are lost. This can be particularly useful at night, in bad weather and when people are buried in snow.

Some dogs work by following a ground scent. Unfortunately this means that if a person is lost and has walked around in circles, the dog will also track these circles. Other dogs work with air scent. This is better as the dogs then go directly to the lost people.

Although many successful mountain rescues take place each year, there are, inevitably, times when people cannot be rescued alive.

13 July 1990

Giant blanket of snow buries Pik Lenin

Forty-three mountaineers are missing, feared dead, after a giant avalanche buried a camp 5200 metres up on Pik Lenin in Russia.

Glossary

alga   a simple green plant; the green slime in a pond is an alga

crust   the solid skin around the Earth

freezing point   the temperature at which liquid becomes a solid; the freezing point for water is zero degrees centigrade

friction   a force caused when two things rub together

fungus   something that gets food from living on rotting material; a mushroom is a fungus

molten   molten rock is rock that has melted and become a liquid

mountain range   a strip of mountains

oxygen   a gas in the air that animals and plants need to survive

summit   the highest point of a mountain

Index

abseiling 17, 19
alga 11
Alps 2, 4, 5
altitude 22
Andes 2, 4 ,5 ,24
Asia 5
Atlas Mountains 2
avalanche 25–26, 30

block mountain 4, 6

canyoning 17
climbing 12–16, 17, 20, 29
crampons 13, 15
cross-country skiing 17

dogs 30

fold mountain 4, 5
fungus 11

Great Dividing Range 2

Haston, Dougal 16
Highlands 4
Himalayas 2, 3, 4, 5, 16, 24
hypothermia 29

ice axe 13, 15
India 5

karabiners 13

lichen 7, 8,11

Mauna Kea 3
Mount Everest 3, 5, 21
Mount Snowdon 12
mountain biking 17, 20
mountain goat 8
mountain rescue 27–30
mountain sport 17–20

Olympus Mons 3

Pik Lenin 30
plants 7, 10, 25
Poppen, Sherman 18
ptarmigan 9

rock crawler 8
Rockies 2, 24

skiing 17
snowboarding 18
snow leopard 9
survival 29

tobogganing 17

volcanic mountain 4, 6

weather 21–26, 27, 30
Whillans, Don 16